HOW? WHO? WHAT? WHEN? WHERE? WHY?

Questions
kids
ask

ABOUT
FARAWAY PLACES

PUBLISHER	Joseph R. DeVarennes	
PUBLICATION DIRECTOR	Kenneth H. Pearson	
ADVISORS	Roger Aubin	
	Robert Furlonger	
EDITORIAL SUPERVISOR	Jocelyn Smyth	
PRODUCTION MANAGER	Ernest Homewood	
PRODUCTION ASSISTANTS	Martine Gingras	Kathy Kishimoto
	Catherine Gordon	Peter Thomlison
CONTRIBUTORS	Alison Dickie	Nancy Prasad
	Bill Ivy	Lois Rock
	Jacqueline Kendel	Merebeth Switzer
	Anne Langdon	Dave Taylor
	Sheila Macdonald	Alison Tharen
	Susan Marshall	Donna Thomson
	Pamela Martin	Pam Young
	Colin McCance	
SENIOR EDITOR	Robin Rivers	
EDITORS	Brian Cross	Ann Martin
	Anne Louise Mahoney	Mayta Tannenbaum
PUBLICATION ADMINISTRATOR	Anna Good	
ART AND DESIGN	Richard Comely	Ronald Migliore
	Robert B. Curry	Penelope Moir
	George Elliott	Marion Stuck
	Marilyn James	Bill Suddick
	Robert Johanssen	Sue Wilkinson

Canadian Cataloguing in Publication Data

Main entry under title:

Questions kids ask about faraway places

(Questions kids ask; 24)
ISBN 0-7172-2563-1

1. Anthropo-geography—Miscellanea—Juvenile literature.
2. World History—Miscellanea—Juvenile literature.
3. Children's questions and answers.
I. Smyth, Jocelyn.   II. Comely, Richard.   III. Series.

GF48.Q48 1988   j909   C89-093173-9

Questions Kids Ask . . . about FARAWAY PLACES

continued

What is the Bermuda Triangle?

Florida, Bermuda, Puerto Rico: these are favorite places to go for a sunny holiday. However, if you drew a line from one place to the other on a map, you would draw the mysterious Bermuda Triangle.

The Bermuda Triangle is a large expanse of the Atlantic Ocean. In the last hundred years, many ships and airplanes have entered that area and then disappeared. Few of them sent out calls for help before they vanished. Where did they go?

One idea is that sudden storms that spring up sink the ships and make the airplanes crash into the sea. Then the waters of the ocean carry the wreckage far away. The problem is, no one knows for certain. No wonder the Bermuda Triangle is sometimes called the Devil's Triangle.

What is the Taj Mahal?

It's hard to imagine, but one of the world's greatest tourist attractions is a tomb. Each year thousands of people go to Agra, in the north of India, to see this beautiful building.

The Taj Mahal was built by Shah Jahan, emperor of India, for his wife Arjunand Banu Begum after her death in 1629. Overcome with grief, Jahan decided that only a great palace-like structure could serve as her last resting place.

Twenty thousand workers took 17 years to build the enormous, gleaming marble building. A large dome covers the center of the structure and slim minarets, or prayer towers, stand at the corners. The white marble walls are decorated with passages from the Koran, the holy book of Muslims.

Shah Jahan had intended to build his own mausoleum across the river from his wife's, but he died before it was constructed and so was buried with his wife. There they have lain for centuries in the marvel Jahan built for love.

Does anyone live in the Kalahari Desert?

In the southern part of Africa lies the great Kalahari Desert. It is a harsh land of low shrubs and few trees. In the dry months, surface water vanishes, and leaves shrivel and turn to dust. It is here that the San live.

The San are a nomadic people who travel in small bands across the Kalahari. Often the best hunter acts as leader, for he is the most likely to know where to find food and water.

Due to the harsh conditions of the desert, the people cannot grow crops or raise animals. They must always be on the move in search of food. Surprisingly, the desert supplies a large number of edible roots and berries, and animals are hunted for food.

The San use bows and arrows that have been dipped in poison. The poison is slow-acting—a hunter who wounds an animal may have to follow it all day before it dies.

Although their life is a hard one they have often been described as a happy people. But as modern technology opens up the Kalahari Desert to farming and ranching, the San way of life is threatened and may soon vanish altogether.

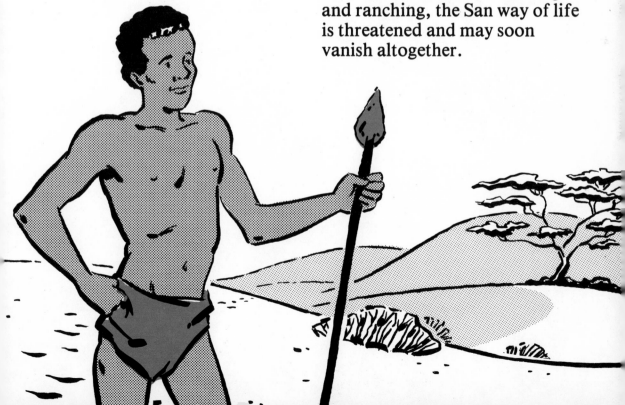

Where is the Great Barrier Reef?

Do you know what coral is? It is formed by tiny sea creatures called polyps. They live together in huge groups. When they die they leave behind tiny skeletons that make a piece of coral.

The waters off the northeast coast of Australia are just right for the creatures that make coral. They have lived there for millions of years. Each tiny creature has added a little bit more coral to the pile until now there is a large barrier called a coral reef in the ocean, just a little way out from shore. It is the biggest reef in the world and is called the Great Barrier Reef. It stretches for 2000 kilometres (1250 miles).

The coral is blue, green, purple, red and yellow. In the sheltered channel between the reef and the shore, brightly colored fish dart about and exotic sea plants wave their long arms in the blue-green water.

No wonder people come from all over the world to admire this fantastic sea garden.

What is the smallest country in the world?

Try to picture an area no bigger than ten football fields. This is about the size of the Vatican, the smallest independent state in the world. It lies inside the city of Rome, Italy, and takes up an area of only 44 hectares (109 acres).

The Vatican is the headquarters of the Roman Catholic Church, and the leader of its government is the pope. Even though the Vatican is the smallest state in the world, it is here that you will find the world's largest Christian church—St. Peter's Basilica.

Only about 1000 people live in the Vatican, but it has its own telephone system, post office, radio station, banking system, postage stamps, daily newspaper and currency!

DID YOU KNOW . . . the world's largest town is Mount Isa, a mining community in northern Australia. It is 40 979 square kilometres (15 822 square miles) . . . 50 times the size of New York City!

Which city has the most people?

The most populous city in the world is Mexico City, Mexico. There were over 18 million people living there in 1985, and the population is still growing at a rate of over 12 000 people each day. Tokyo has the second largest population, with just over 11 million.

Tokyo's metropolitan area—the area surrounding the city—has over 28 million people. That is more than the entire population of Canada!

Where is Timbuktu?

There is an old saying about going "from here to Timbuktu," which means a place that is very far away. Many people think that Timbuktu is an imaginary place, but it is a real city on the southern edge of the Sahara Desert in Africa.

It is inhabited by three groups of people—all Muslims. They are mainly involved in trading because Timbuktu is on a large river, the Niger. This river carries goods to the desert dwellers. At the same time, it carries south their main trade item: salt.

What is a pagoda?

A pagoda is a tall, slender building made of brick, wood or stone. Found in many Asian countries including India, China, Japan and Korea, pagodas look like fancy wedding cakes with many tiers, or levels. Each level is smaller than the one below it and has its own roof with large graceful eaves that turn upwards.

Pagodas were first built as places to keep religious relics, but today they are also used as tombs, shrines and memorials.

DID YOU KNOW . . . people used to believe that the pagoda was a symbol of the universe. The four columns at the corners of a pagoda were believed to be the pillars of the sky.

What is a ricksha?

The jinrikisha, or ricksha as tourists usually call it, is a popular way to travel in China and Japan. It is a light two-wheeled cart with two long handlebars attached to the bottom. Some rickshas have hoods to protect passengers from rain and sunlight. The driver places himself between the handlebars and runs down the street, pulling his passengers who sit in the cart. It must be a very exhausting job!

Today, pedicabs, which are like large tricycles, are used more often than rickshas. The driver simply pedals his passengers around.

So if you're ever in Asia and yell ''Taxi,'' don't be surprised if a ricksha runner or a tricycle pedaler pulls up and says ''Hop in''!

Was the Sahara always a desert?

Stretched across the top of Africa is the largest desert in the world—the Sahara. It is so large that it could cover half of North America.

Today the Sahara is a land of rock and gravel—only 20 percent of it is covered with sand. The weather is hot and dry and water is very scarce. Less than 12 centimetres (5 inches) of rain falls each year. Some parts don't even get that much!

But the Sahara wasn't always a desert. It looked a lot different 10 000 years ago, during the Great Ice Age. There were many lakes and streams and enough rain fell to support forests and grasslands. Herds of giraffes and elephants roamed. It was a rich and fertile land.

Then, about 4000 years ago, the climate changed. The weather became drier and slowly the land turned to desert.

Now only the dried up river and lake beds remain to tell the story of how green this great desert once was.

LEMONADE

DID YOU KNOW . . . people once believed the source of the White Nile was the mysterious Mountains of the Moon.

What is the longest river in the world?

It is the Nile—which flows more than 6400 kilometres (4000 miles) from the rain forests of central Africa, through the hot Egyptian desert, to the Mediterranean Sea. The Nile starts out as two rivers. The White Nile starts at Lake Victoria Nyanza, in central Africa. From there it flows north, until it is met by the Blue Nile. The Blue Nile rises in the mountains of Ethiopia, and every year it is swollen by heavy rains. This water overflows the banks of the river far away in Egypt.

Near Cairo and the pyramids that overlook the river, begins the vast Nile Delta. The force of the river is lost in countless channels and reed plains before two channels finally reach the sea.

What is Easter Island famous for?

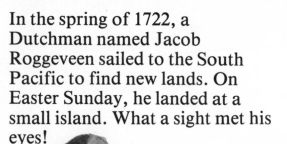

In the spring of 1722, a Dutchman named Jacob Roggeveen sailed to the South Pacific to find new lands. On Easter Sunday, he landed at a small island. What a sight met his eyes!

Centuries before, the people who lived on the island had carved great stone statues of their chiefs. They cut them out of the volcanic rock of the island using simple tools of stone. Next, the people dragged the statues into position on wooden sledges. Finally, they levered the statues into place by pushing them up with huge wooden poles.

There are over 600 statues on Easter Island and most of them weigh over 20 metric tons. They range from 3 metres (10 feet) to 11 metres (37 feet) tall.

What are the Galapagos Islands famous for?

Off the coast of South America in the Pacific Ocean is a group of 16 islands. Known as the Galapagos Islands, they are actually ancient volcanoes whose peaks rise high above the waves.

The Galapagos Islands are famous because of the many unusual creatures that live on them. For example, there are giant land tortoises (*galápagos*, in Spanish), flightless cormorants and large marine iguanas that are over a metre (3 feet) long. These are not found anywhere else in the world. The naturalist Charles Darwin visited the islands in 1835 and studied the distinctive plants and animals. He helped to make the Galapagos Islands famous by writing about them when he returned to England.

DID YOU KNOW . . . the Galapagos Islands are also called the Enchanted Isles. In days gone by, pirates used to bury treasure there.

17

Where is the Bridge of Sighs?

The Bridge of Sighs is a famous landmark in Venice, Italy. It crosses the canal between the Doge's Palace and the state prison. It's called the Bridge of Sighs because it was once used by prisoners who, if found guilty at the palace trial, were led back over the bridge to be executed. As you can imagine, a lot of unhappy people probably sighed many times while crossing it.

The bridge was built in the late 1500s by the Italian architect Antonio Contino.

Where is Mecca?

Near the Red Sea, in the Sirat mountains of Saudi Arabia, lies the city of Mecca. Mecca is the birthplace of one of the world's great religions—Islam. Muhammad, the founder of Islam, was born here in 570. Muslims, the followers of Islam, believe that one day the angel Gabriel came to Muhammad with a message from God. Later he received other messages, and these formed the basis of the Koran, the holy book of Islam.

Making a pilgrimage to Mecca is one of the principles of being a Muslim. Each year over a million people go there, but only Muslims are allowed to enter this holy city. Every day when Muslims say their prayers they face in the direction of the city of Mecca.

What is the Wailing Wall?

Jerusalem is special to the Jews because much of their history took place in and around that city. Since ancient times, their holy Temple has been there.

The Western Wall, or Wailing Wall, in Jerusalem is in fact part of the original temple built by King Solomon. People go to the wall to attend religious services and to pray. They may weep as they remember the history of their people and the sufferings they had to go through. As a result, the wall is known as the Wailing Wall.

DID YOU KNOW . . . there is a story that once, a small boy in Holland saw a trickle of water coming through a dyke. He knew that the land would be flooded if the water from the sea broke through the dyke, so he held his finger over the leak until someone came to fix it.

Why are the Netherlands so flat?

Many parts of the Netherlands are very flat. These lands are called the polders and they are flat because they were once marshes. The Dutch decided to drain the polders so they could grow crops in the fertile soil.

They cut canals to take the water away and built strong walls called dykes to stop sea water rushing back onto the low land. They also built windmills so that they could use wind power to pump the water into the canals.

What is the highest place in the world?

The top of Mount Everest is the highest place in the world. On a sunny day its peak can be seen from as far as 160 kilometres (100 miles) away!

Mount Everest is part of the Himalayas—a mountain range on the border between Tibet and Nepal. The people of Tibet call Mount Everest "chomolungma," which means Goddess Mother of the World. It is easy to see how it got this name. Mount Everest rises 8848 metres (29 028 feet) above sea level. That's about 9 kilometres (5-1/2 miles) high! The summit of Everest reaches two-thirds of the way through the earth's atmosphere.

What is the deepest lake in the world?

The deepest lake in the world is Lake Baikal, in the eastern part of the Soviet Union. Surrounded by mountains, Baikal is a long, narrow lake, which is more than 1.6 kilometres (a mile) deep at its deepest point. Baikal holds a huge amount of water: one-fifth of the earth's fresh water. The lake is full of fish, including many unusual types found nowhere else. Baikal also has the world's only fresh-water seals, as well as a great variety of waterfowl and seabirds. Unfortunately, logging in the surrounding mountains and large mills on its shores have led to serious pollution problems. The Soviet government is now trying to protect the region.

!

A LONG WAY TO LAKE BOTTOM

Why is the Dead Sea dead?

The Dead Sea is not really a sea. It is a huge lake in a low-lying hollow between Israel and Jordan. Rivers flow into the Dead Sea but none flow out of it. The only way water gets out is by evaporating in the hot sun.

But the little bits of solid that are in the water can't evaporate. More and more bits are left behind as the water evaporates.

A lot of salt flows into the Dead Sea. Over the years, more and more salt has been left behind as water has evaporated. For many hundreds of years, the water has been so salty that no fish or plants can live in it. That is why people say that it is dead.

DID YOU KNOW . . . the Dead Sea is seven times saltier than the ocean.

What is the biggest lake in the world?

The largest inland body of water in the world is a great salt lake 28 metres (92 feet) below sea level called the Caspian Sea. In fact, it isn't a sea at all, nor does it have an outlet to the sea. Because it was once linked to the ocean, however, seals live in its waters. This lake covers 372 000 square kilometres (143 630 square miles) and is almost as big as the state of California. Surrounded on three sides by the Soviet Union with its southern shore against Iran, this huge lake is shrinking—the rivers which empty into it are bringing in less water than it loses by evaporation. Because the water of the Caspian is only one-third as salty as ocean waters, both fresh-water and salt-water fish can be found there.

Which is the world's largest rain forest?

A huge river called the Amazon winds through a large part of South America. Many other rivers flow into it. On the swampy land along the river grows a forest so thick that it is almost impossible to cut a path. The branches of the trees are so entwined that the sunlight cannot reach down to the forest floor. This is the Amazon rain forest. It is dark . . . and dangerous!

Alligators and piranhas
lurk in the rivers. There are
exotic creatures, too: brightly colored
parrots and giant butterflies.
Unfortunately, people are
clearing away some of the forest to make
farmland. Scientists and other people are worried that this
could have a disastrous effect and are trying to preserve the
Amazon rain forest.

What is Big Ben?

Big Ben is a huge bell in the clock tower of the Houses of Parliament in London, England. The bell rang for the first time in 1859.

Big Ben is certainly big. It is 2.3 metres (7.5 feet) high, 2.7 metres (9 feet) across and weighs 12 000 kilograms (26 000 pounds).

The bell was named after Sir Benjamin Hall, the tall and chubby commissioner of works who was nicknamed Big Ben by the members of the British Parliament.

When Big Ben rings, you can't help but listen!

What is the Eiffel Tower?

In 1889 the city of Paris in France held a huge fair. People came from all over the world. In order to show off how modern they were, the French built a tower that was the tallest in the world. The person who designed it was an engineer named Alexandre Gustave Eiffel, and they named it after him. The Eiffel Tower is an elegant framework of iron bars that soars from a broad base to a narrow tip. It is 300 metres (984 feet) tall.

Visitors can climb or take an elevator to one of the viewing platforms on the tower and enjoy a view of Paris.

DID YOU KNOW . . . the CN Tower in Toronto now holds the record as the tallest freestanding tower in the world. It is nearly twice as high as the Eiffel Tower.

Why does the Leaning Tower of Pisa lean?

Have you ever seen pictures of the Leaning Tower of Pisa? It looks so natural to us to see the tower lean that it is hard to imagine that it was meant to be just like any other tower—straight!

The Leaning Tower is in Pisa, Italy. It is made entirely of white marble and it is eight storeys tall.

The Tower took 200 years to build. It was begun in 1174 but, when the first three storeys were finished, it started to tip. Why? The tower was being built on sand—not solid ground!

Sand is made of tiny grains. Between the grains are tiny spaces. The grains of sand move and settle into these spaces. Whatever is built on sand shifts and settles as the sand moves.

The Tower of Pisa is still tipping—another millimetre every year.

What are catacombs?

Catacombs are underground tunnels cut into the rock. They were used as places to lay the dead. Many ancient peoples built catacombs under their cities. In times of danger, they might flee to the catacombs for safety.

There are catacombs in North Africa, Germany, France and Malta but the most famous ones are the 40 in Rome. They were used for religious services and burials.

Where is the largest active volcano?

In Ecuador, in South America, a beautiful, cone-shaped peak rises 5900 metres (19 350 feet) into the air and it is part of the Andes mountains. Ice and snow shimmer on the mountain sides, but deep inside, liquid rock from the fiery core of the earth boils and churns. Clouds of steam flow constantly out of its crater.

This is Cotopaxi, the world's highest volcano. It has erupted many times in the last few centuries. Boiling rock called lava poured out of the peak and flowed over the ice fields. Then terrible mud slides slithered down the mountain. The most recent eruption was in 1928.

Where do reindeer come from?

Did you think that reindeer came from Santa's home at the North Pole? Not so! The traditional home of the reindeer is a land in northern Europe—Lapland. Here, the winter lasts nine months of the year and the land is bleak. Lapland stretches across northern Norway, Sweden, Finland and part of the Soviet Union.

The people who live there are called Lapps. They follow the reindeer herds and use them as we use cows: for milk, meat, hides and other useful products. They also use reindeer to pull sleighs. The reindeer's wide feet act like snowshoes so that the animal does not sink deep into the snow but runs over it lightly.

However, no Lapp has yet managed to train a reindeer to pull a sleigh up into the sky!

DID YOU KNOW . . . from September to March the South Pole is tilted toward the sun. At that time, the North Pole remains dark and the lands around it have long, dark nights and only a few hours of daylight.

Where is the world's largest island?

If you don't count Australia and Antarctica (which are classified as continents anyway), then Greenland is the world's largest island. With a total area of about 2 175 600 square kilometres (840 000 square miles), it's almost nine times as big as Great Britain. Almost all of Greenland is covered by a sheet of ice that's nearly 1.5 kilometres (a mile) thick in places, so its population is small relative to the size of the island.

Nevertheless, more than 50 000 people like Greenland well enough to live there. There are animals there, too—including polar bears, wolves, musk oxen and caribou. The waters around Greenland are full of fish, which is how most of the people make their living, but sailing in those waters is dangerous, because they are full of great icebergs and it is very foggy.

Index